CELEBRATING THE FAMILY NAME OF CLARK

Celebrating the Family Name of Clark

Walter the Educator

Silent King Books
a WhichHead Entertainment Imprint

Copyright © 2024 by Walter the Educator

All rights reserved. No part of this book may be reproduced in any manner whatsoever without written permission except in the case of brief quotations embodied in critical articles and reviews.

First Printing, 2024

Disclaimer

This book is a literary work; the story is not about specific persons, locations, situations, and/or circumstances unless mentioned in a historical context. Any resemblance to real persons, locations, situations, and/or circumstances is coincidental. This book is for entertainment and informational purposes only. The author and publisher offer this information without warranties expressed or implied. No matter the grounds, neither the author nor the publisher will be accountable for any losses, injuries, or other damages caused by the reader's use of this book. The use of this book acknowledges an understanding and acceptance of this disclaimer.

Celebrating the Family Name of Clark is a memory book that belongs to the Celebrating Family Name Book Series by Walter the Educator. Collect them all and more books at WaltertheEducator.com

USE THE EXTRA SPACE TO DOCUMENT YOUR FAMILY MEMORIES THROUGHOUT THE YEARS

CLARK

In the quiet dawn, where shadows play,

Celebrating the Family Name of

Clark

And morning whispers of a new day,

The name of Clark begins to rise,

A timeless tale beneath the skies.

From fields of green to city streets,

Wherever life and journey meets,

The Clark name stands, a pillar tall,

A beacon bright through it all.

With hands that build and minds that dream,

The Clarks pursue a steady stream,

Of hopes and visions, strong and clear,

A family bound by love sincere.

Through history's pages, worn and old,

The name of Clark, with stories bold,

Has carved its path in stone and earth,

A name of honor, strength, and worth.

Celebrating the Family Name of

Clark

The Clarks have walked through fire and rain,

With steadfast hearts that bear no stain,

In every challenge, every fight,

They've shown the world their boundless might.

In every child, a spark is found,

Of Clark's enduring, sacred ground,

A legacy that lights the way,

Through darkest night and brightest day.

The winds may shift, the tides may turn,

But still the Clark fires brightly burn,

In every heart, in every hand,

A unity that time has spanned.

Through laughter shared and tears once cried,

The Clark name flows like an endless tide,

A river deep, with waters pure,

Celebrating the Family Name of

Clark

A bond that nothing can obscure.

In every corner of the earth,

The Clark name echoes, rich in worth,

With roots that stretch and branches wide,

A family strong, a trusted guide.

The Clarks have sailed on oceans vast,

With sails that hold against the blast,

Through tempests wild and calmest seas,

Celebrating the Family Name of

Clark

They journey on with hearts at ease.

ABOUT THE CREATOR

Walter the Educator is one of the pseudonyms for Walter Anderson. Formally educated in Chemistry, Business, and Education, he is an educator, an author, a diverse entrepreneur, and he is the son of a disabled war veteran. "Walter the Educator" shares his time between educating and creating. He holds interests and owns several creative projects that entertain, enlighten, enhance, and educate, hoping to inspire and motivate you. Follow, find new works, and stay up to date with Walter the Educator™ at WaltertheEducator.com

www.ingramcontent.com/pod-product-compliance
Lightning Source LLC
LaVergne TN
LVHW012051070526
838201LV00082B/3907